TOD INLET

TOD INLET
A HEALING PLACE

Gwen Curry

Gwen Curry.

Rocky Mountain Books
www.rmbooks.com

Library and Archives Canada Cataloguing in Publication
Curry, Gwen, author, photographer
    Tod Inlet : a healing place / Gwen Curry.

Includes bibliographical references.
Issued in print and electronic formats.

ISBN 978-1-77160-076-7 (pbk.).—ISBN 978-1-77160-077-4 (epub).—
ISBN 978-1-77160-078-1 (pdf)

    1. Tod Inlet (B.C.). 2. Tod Inlet (B.C.)—Pictorial works. 3. Gowlland Tod
Provincial Park (B.C.). 4. Gowlland Tod Provincial Park (B.C.)—Pictorial works.
I. Title.

FC3815.G68C87 2015   333.78'30971128   C2015-901006-3   C2015-901007-1

Cover Design: Chyla Cardinal
Interior Design: Frances Hunter

Printed in Canada

Rocky Mountain Books acknowledges the financial support for its publishing
program from the Government of Canada through the Canada Book Fund (CBF)
and the Canada Council for the Arts, and from the province of British Columbia
through the British Columbia Arts Council and the Book Publishing Tax Credit.

This book was produced using FSC®-certified, acid-free paper, processed
chlorine free and printed with vegetable-based inks.

Contents

FOREWORD

The beauty of Tod Inlet, "Place of the Blue Grouse," lies not only in the matrix of its firs, ferns, cedars and maples, but also in its underlying resilience and our commitment to have this place remain a place of refuge and healing. The Inlet, which is described eloquently in Gwen Curry's words and images, could so easily have become a resort and housing development for a culture that mistakes wants for needs. Instead, the echoes of stream, wind and birdsong, the splash of heron finding prey and otter scrambling over rock continue to reside alongside the Inlet's memory of steam whistle and breaking rock.

The history of this place is ever present. In the following pages you will share the layers of stories told with grace and exquisite images. The colour, texture, sounds and shapes of cultures and communities are interwoven seamlessly by an artist of profound sensitivity. With keen eyes and an inquisitive mind, Gwen continues the shapes of past and present in careful detail, always with an overarching sensitivity to life yearning for itself. She simultaneously captures the wide-angle shot of "before time" and the refined view of the smallest seedling of spring. Her gift of vision is evident throughout this testimony to a special place. Take heart from her musings. She gives us not only a story we can bear witness to, but also shares the wisdom unearthed from this place for our daily mindfulness. Thank you, Gwen.

— Nikki Wright, *Executive Director, SeaChange Marine Conservation Society*

INTRODUCTION

In the four decades that I've walked the trail to Tod Inlet I can't pretend to know the place. Its apparent stillness mocks me. I can name a plant, sit in reverie on one of its banks or be in awe of a leaf shot through with sunlight, but the pervasive intelligence of this place is rooted in centuries of being. Tod Inlet has been a place of refuge for hundreds, if not thousands, of years, but few are aware of its history. Six years ago I began a photographic homage to the Inlet and its surroundings. Initially its beauty and serenity were all I needed to keep me focused on my project, but its history kept intruding and I finally began to tell its story.

Tod Inlet curves away from Saanich Inlet at Brentwood Bay, 25 minutes north of Victoria, and creates a half moat around Butchart Gardens. The park entrance is easy to miss – the only indication of its location is the line of cars snugged under the maples and ocean spray bushes at the side of Wallace Drive. This section of Gowlland Tod Provincial Park is a forested trail following Tod Creek to the sea. For centuries it was the home of the W̱SÁNEĆ (Saanich) people. This sheltered Inlet provided an abundance of food, fresh water, building materials, utensils and clothing as well as a place for spiritual practice. In the early part of the twentieth century a small company town grew on its shores. Houses, a railway, a clay mill, a factory and a dock for steamships were built. The Vancouver Portland Cement Company hired Chinese and Indian

Aerial view of Tod Inlet, with Butchart Gardens top right.

workers who were seeking employment in Canada. By 1921 the cement company had exhausted the limestone quarries and Jennie Butchart had begun her ambitious gardening project, saying, "We have made something ugly, now let's make it beautiful again." The factory carried on for many years as a tile and ceramic pot manufacturer and Tod Village was still inhabited into the 1960s. Almost all of the buildings have been demolished, but concrete and iron are not easily disposed of and reminders of the past confront the walker everywhere: shell middens spill into the sea, fruit trees and garden flowers mingle with indigenous plants, and century-old industrial relics litter the creek, the forest and the Inlet. But despite the ravages of the past century, Tod Inlet retains a spirit of peace and renewal.

My relationship with Tod Inlet began in the 1970s. There were a few structures not yet demolished and treasure hunters had picked over the remains of the Chinese workers' village. It had been only a few years since the last houses of Tod Village were razed and almost a century since the W̱SÁNEĆ people had been able to enjoy their former hunting and fishing grounds.

It is not my intention to create a definitive history of the Inlet, but rather to wander down its trails, noticing present-day Tod Inlet while unearthing glimpses into its past. This book is a visual homage to the Inlet's natural and constructed beauty and often the intersection of the two.

The area covered includes the Wallace Drive entrance to Tod Inlet, bordered on the south by the base of the Partridge Hills and to the northwest by the fenced boundary of Butchart Gardens – perhaps 60 hectares of this 1200 hectare park that extends down Finlayson Arm almost to Goldstream Park.

I have capitalized the word "Inlet" throughout the book as a sign of my affection for it. Although the book encompasses the seasons of one year, the images are a compilation of six years of photography.

···SPRING···

S PRING RUSHES INTO TOD INLET, refusing to obey the calendar. In late February and early March while the rest of the country slumbers, no buds quickening, it is impossible to keep up with the changes here. Indigenous and introduced species are all awakening. The Indian plum bushes are sprinkled with thumb-sized floral arrangements of green and white, and the ocean spray bushes have new shoots the size of sesame seeds. A balsam shines with three inches of soft, lime-green growth at the tips of its branches, and the first spears of skunk cabbages push up out of the dark soil of a pond. This plant is a sign of fertile soil – perhaps Tod Inlet's early name "Skunk Hollow" isn't as demeaning as it sounds. Masses of watercress will soon share the same shallow pool, and hardy violets will bloom on the perimeter of this artesian spring. Daffodils planted many years ago are nestled in the dry winter bushes, their flowers encased in green sheaths, waiting for the next sunny day to unfurl. The introduced holly bushes have minuscule flower bunches that resemble stems of Brussels sprouts when viewed through my macro lens, and a sprinkling of prairie crocus overlooks the still water above the dam.

Mature alder trees form a backdrop for the skunk cabbage at the spring.

I walk to the Inlet. The tide is low and my shoes sink into the foreshore as I scan the beach for artifacts. A rectangle of concrete the size of a fisherman's skiff rests in the silt, refusing to disintegrate, studded with cockles and oysters. The concrete relic and the shell-fish are both made of lime – the former aided by the hand of man, while the latter needed no such inter-ference. I spy a teapot, part of its spout missing. It resembles a tiny brown Betty and sits on a shelf that is part granite outcropping and part industrial debris. How has it survived the ebb and flow of four daily tides for 70 years or more? Other pieces of chinaware litter the shoreline, some looking decidedly British, and others exquisitely oriental. A plate bears the sig-nature "Grindley" below a caricature of an old sail-ing ship. The design is Cream Petal. Pieces of glass are cast with ornate patterns usually reserved for crystal. A shard of pottery is crazed on its silvery exterior, but the orange rust has made it gaudy. The lid to the teapot sits beside an ancient leg bone from a pig – pork and tea from a century-old meal in the Chinese workers' village. A chain the width of a man's fist has morphed into an organic form, its links now rigid and bound together by a growth of barnacles. Nearby sits a small sack of cement. The sack is long gone, but the stress lines from the fabric are still visible, making it look like a petrified pillow.

A few months later, I take advantage of another low tide and squelch my way across the sloping beach looking for new or familiar treasures. I come upon a small landslide about 25 feet wide that has slumped onto the shore, blocking my path. I realize that this is the location of the glass and pottery shards I had been photographing months before. Everything is buried except the pillow of Portland cement, sitting there like the ignored museum piece that it is.

At the beginning of the twentieth century, Tod Inlet was the site of the Vancouver Portland Cement Company, in production from 1904 to 1921. It is a testament to the fecundity of nature that most visitors experience this portion of Gowlland Tod Provincial Park as a calming, even spiritual place. But this Eden fulfilled its role in the industrial birth of British Columbia: beneath the towering trees were solid deposits of limestone.

In the nineteenth century, kilns were built extensively in Great Britain and gave rise to a type of artisan called a lime burner. This early cement was inferior to Portland cement, a more complex product that was continually being refined during the century, first in

England and then the United States and Canada. Its name derives from its similarity to Portland stone, a building material quarried on the Isle of Portland in Dorset, England. John Greig, one of the first landowners at Tod Inlet, was undoubtedly a lime burner in his native Scotland before being employed by the Hudson's Bay Company and working his way to the coast of British Columbia. Greig had already owned two quarries and kilns in the Victoria area before his purchase of the Tod Inlet property. Lime Bay in Esquimalt was the site of one of these quarries. In 1869 Greig purchased 219 acres at Tod Inlet from Captain Thomas Pritchard, a wealthy Victoria businessman and avid orchardist. Greig, known as "Greig the Fiddler," spent the next 15 years quarrying and burning limestone here, as well as tending his own farm and orchard. He and his wife, Margaret Goudie, whose mother was a First Nations woman, raised ten children and in 1884 granted the property to two sons, William and James, who eventually sold it to the Saanich Lime Company in 1890. It might have been appropriate to name the Inlet after Greig, but he is memorialized by Greig Avenue in Brentwood Bay and was not a public figure as John Tod was.

Tod, also a Scotsman, was born near Loch Lomond in 1794 and came to the colony of Vancouver Island to work for the Hudson's Bay Company, eventually buying a 100-acre farm in what is now Oak Bay. After retirement from the HBC in 1851, he was appointed to the first legislative council in Victoria. He delighted in books, music and conversation and was known as

"a consummate story-teller ... a character and a much married man" according to Charles Lillard in a series he wrote for the *Times Colonist* on Victoria's early history. A contemporary described Tod as a man whose "intellect was as fresh and inquisitive as that of a promising young college lad ... and strangely enough in one of his speculative genius [sic] he excelled all men I have listened to in unaffected graphic narration, without scene-painting or counterfeit." In 1878 Hubert Howe Bancroft, author of a 39-volume history of western North America, described his contemporary, John Tod, in old age:

> Sitting in an armchair, leaning on his cane, or walking up and down the room, his deep-set eyes blazing with the renewed fires of old-time excitements; his thin hair standing in electric attention, he recited with rapidity midst furious gesticulations story after story, one scene calling up another, until his present was wet with the sweat of the past.

John Tod, a spiritualist, might today be referred to as a psychic medium.

Captain George Henry Richards named Tod Creek in honour of John Tod in 1858 when he was surveying the coast in HMS *Plumper*, a steam sloop of the British Navy. The name "Tod Creek" originally described the area from Senanus Island to Tod Inlet, including Brentwood Bay.

In 1904, when the Vancouver Portland Cement Company purchased the property surrounding Tod Inlet, it was owned by Peter Fernie. The manager of the new company, Robert Pim Butchart, and his wife, Jennie, moved into Mr. Fernie's cottage.

Tiny Senanus Island, a formal burial site for the W̱SÁNEĆ people, sits off Tod Inlet in Brentwood Bay.

Tod Inlet curves around Butchart Gardens. Lower left is Butchart's Cove.

Robert Butchart, the son of a ship chandler, was born in Owen Sound, Ontario, in 1856. He had been involved in two other cement companies prior to coming to Tod Inlet. Both were located at Shallow Lake, Ontario, although they had different names. The first proved unsuccessful for all involved and ended with litigation, investment losses and inferior cement. Butchart might have given up after this venture, but he regrouped with new investors and tried again with the Owen Sound Portland Cement Company. Butchart travelled to England and returned with a superintendent, a miller, a burner and a very necessary piece of equipment – a new rotary kiln. His gamble paid off, and the new company mastered the art of making quality Portland cement, though one last hurdle remained. Butchart and his company had introduced a new method for shipment: sacks. Until this time the industry had used 374-pound wooden barrels to transport Portland cement, and prospective buyers were leery of this new packaging weighing in at just 88 pounds. Butchart and company were ahead of their competition, as this change from barrels to bags had only just begun in the United States as a response to shipping by rail instead of steamship. The city of Toronto placed the first order, and when it declared the cement an excellent product, more orders ensued. Ten years had elapsed since the failure of Butchart's first cement plant.

Nine years later, in 1904, a third company was formed at Tod Inlet with E.R. Woods as president, Robert Butchart as managing director and H.A. Ross as treasurer. This was the first cement plant in western Canada and supplied the Portland for such projects as the Jordan River dam, the Powell River dam and the generating plant at Brentwood Bay. Previously, concrete had to be shipped to the west coast from England via the Horn of South America, as the Panama Canal was not completed until 1914. There was a ready and waiting market for the Vancouver Portland Cement Company, and it eventually serviced the whole coast from California to British Columbia.

Tod Inlet was Butchart's third plant (of seven) and of course his most famous due to his industrious wife. Jennie Butchart was a talented and adventurous woman. She enjoyed riding in hot air balloons and early airplanes and was a trained chemist who assisted with the laboratory tests crucial to the production of Portland cement. Only five years after the start of the plant, the main quarry was exhausted and Jennie Butchart was busy restoring what would become the Sunken Gardens. She had wanted to be an artist and found an outlet in the transformation of the spent limestone quarries.

An electric pole for the Vancouver Portland Cement Company is reclaimed by the forest.

Century-old concrete pilings once supported the wharf where steamships docked at the Vancouver Portland Cement Company.

The original cement factory road leads from Butchart Gardens down to the Inlet.

I WALK DOWN THE OLD ROAD that still connects Butchart Gardens to Tod Inlet. In the tangled forest to my left, hazes of pink and white blossoms identify plum trees that have gone wild. A hundred feet farther along I meet the main trail and turn right, down the company road that leads straight to the cement factory site. A canopy of firs and cedars forms an arch overhead. I pass a few culturally modified trees – a term for cedar trees from which First Nations people have stripped a length of bark to use for weaving and rope making. A straight horizontal cut about a foot wide is notched into the tree. The piece of bark from that notch is lifted vertically until it reaches a vanishing point eight to ten feet above, forming a long, thin triangle. The cutline doesn't encircle the trunk, which maintains the flow of sap and leaves the tree healthy.

Recently a group of local Native weavers were planning a trip to Jordan River to locate suitable cedar trees for stripping. A family member informed the weavers that they had traditional rights at Gowlland Tod Provincial Park. They notified the park warden of their plan and it was agreed they could harvest in the park. The warden stipulated that they should choose trees that were off the trail or take the bark from the side facing away from the trail. This request seemed an affront, so today park users have a visual reminder of the needs and history of the first people of Tod Inlet. It is impossible to imagine Coast Salish culture without the cedar tree, which was used for houses, canoes, food vessels, clothes, baskets, hats, ropes, mats, carvings and ceremonial items – the list seems endless.

John Elliott Sr., a member of the Tsartlip Band, remembers fishing for spring salmon at Tod Creek in 1962, when he was just a boy. Today he teaches at the Tsartlip ȽÁU, WELṈEW̱ Tribal High School, where he and the late Earl Claxton Sr., a member of the Tsawout Band, worked for 28 years reviving the SENĆOŦEN language. They both continued the research initiated by John Elliott's father, Dave Elliott Sr., Ray Sam and other elders. John Elliott Sr. is an artist, cultural historian and linguist, and his classroom has a fresh, tea-like scent from the various bulrush and cedar weavings that line the countertops. Tod Inlet is part of his classroom too – there, his students harvest cedar and weave rope while learning about their heritage. He tells me the name of Tod Creek in the SENĆOŦEN language: W̱EĆEĆE. It translates as "The Little Awakener." Cold-water bathing was (and is) practised in winter for strengthening, often in the early morning before daybreak. Coming-of-age rituals also used "The Little Awakener." When young boys' voices changed, bathing in the creek served to strengthen the mind so that their nascent sexuality was tempered and the boys wouldn't embarrass their elders. The importance of cold-water bathing for spiritual rebuilding in the W̱SÁNEĆ (Saanich) culture originates from the creation story of SLEMEW – the first man. He was the human spirit of the rain and was lowered down to Tod Inlet in the night. Even the SENĆOŦEN word for water can be translated as "rain after."

For millennia, Tod Inlet, or SṈITȻEȽ (which means "Place of the Blue Grouse"), was a bountiful and weather-safe haven for the W̱SÁNEĆ people. This tiny curve of an Inlet was home to cutthroat and rainbow trout, perch, coho and spring salmon, ling cod, rock cod, herring, octopus, littleneck clams, anchovies, pilchard, sea cucumbers, crab, sole, ducks and geese. On the steep hillsides to the south and the gently rolling land to the north of Tod Inlet, game was plentiful: elk, bear, deer, grouse, wolves and cougars. Women harvested bulrushes from the head of the Inlet. Clams were dug from the shoreline, and salmon were caught from canoes. Herring roe was harvested simply by placing cedar branches in the water so that some of the fish would spawn on it instead of the eelgrass meadows.

Pages 34–35: Dr. John Elliott Sr. and students at SṈITȻEȽ (Tod Inlet). As a result of the language program at the ȽÁU, WELṈEW̱ Tribal School, the W̱SÁNEĆ community has fluent young speakers of SENĆOŦEN. On the following page are cedar trees that have been sustainably stripped of their bark by local W̱SÁNEĆ weavers.

The winter months were a spiritual time for the Saanich people and still are. Societal dancing and initiations took place in the longhouse. Members were sent to SN̲ITȻEȽ to spend time alone: walking, fasting, bathing and seeking inner vision. These scenes sound bucolic, but in the late 1800s First Nation villages were crowded onto small areas of land that could not sustain this semi-nomadic culture. Tod Inlet's history is a microcosm of the history of the North American continent, if not the world. Here, on the Saanich Peninsula, the introduction of colonial diseases decimated an otherwise healthy people. In the first half of the twentieth century there were new sounds on the reserves: coughing, crying and the ever-present crack of hammer to nail as coffins were built, often daily. Even the dead bore the indignity of having to conform to another culture.

Children were forced to attend residential schools that began in 1884. Most were gone by 1948, although the last one was closed as recently as 1996. Almost all of the schools were run by Catholic and Anglican churches under the auspices of the Canadian government. Education was not the priority, as the teachers were barely schooled themselves. Rather, the intended outcome was that the girls would become domestics and the boys would be assimilated as farmers.

Left: William Morris of the Tsartlip Band returns from Tod Inlet in his canoe.

Right: Close-up of a shell midden.

When the children were taken to the schools, their hair was shorn and coated in a powdered chemical (usually DDT). They were forbidden to speak the only language they knew. Frightened children slept on metal cots in long rows. They were undernourished and cold most of the time and many succumbed to influenza, chicken pox, measles and tuberculosis. Government research now estimates that more than half the children died while attending these schools or soon after returning home. If a young girl was raped (usually by a religious leader at the school or a teacher) and became pregnant, she was sent to Vancouver to have the child and then returned to the residential school, alone. Young boys were also sexually abused and then returned to their villages hurt, confused and crippled.

It is a triumph of the human spirit that Native culture today is being remembered and passed on, and Tod Inlet, as a spiritual sanctuary for the W̱SÁNEĆ people, is a part of that rebirth.

A young western garter snake warms itself in the spring sunlight.

A SPRING WIND is rushing down the Inlet today, sounding like a parallel creek in the canopy high above me. At first the cool wind and grey clouds dampen my spirits, but minutes later the sky appears in blue patches, the sun lights up the creek's rapids, and I feel better immediately. A crackling sound on this otherwise muddy pathway alerts me. A magnificent garter snake is moving across the dry maple leaves beside the path, creating the characteristic rustle. I stop, she stops. A second, smaller snake appears. The smaller snake, perhaps 18 inches long, slithers gracefully over last year's leaves, occasionally lifting its head in the air to catch any scent, while the larger snake, at least two feet in length, remains motionless. Her lovely body has lime-green stripes interspersed with dark grey-green markings. These northwestern garter snakes are here to soak up the weak rays of the spring sun, as they have no other way of producing body heat. They have just emerged after wintering in a hibernation ball in an underground pit,

42

and the larger snake will give birth to live young in the middle of summer. These harmless snakes keep the slug population in check and may live to be 12 to 15 years old.

Today, at the spring, the sensual blooms of the skunk cabbage stand like beacons against the black earth. The skeeter bugs are skating across the surface of the water, inching forward with their abbreviated breaststrokes in what appears to be a random pattern. I'm engulfed by the perfume of the *Prunus psardi*, or Japanese plum tree. Its blossoms cascade over the pond, raining a white cloud of confetti on the watercress and the hardy violets. As I breathe in the scent of the plum blossoms, I'm startled by a crashing sound in the dried blackberry bushes nearby. It's all I can do to stay planted, rather than instinctively duck. A furious and equally startled male towhee bursts out of the thicket, warning me with his raspy chirp. He flutters to a nearby branch and perches, looking like a tiny Bernese mountain dog with his vibrant patches of black, rust and white feathers. Tod Creek's inhabitants are all in mating mode on this spring day.

Three young mothers pass me, four children in tow, one in a carriage. The little boy has boots on and walks purposefully into the spring and the skunk cabbage. A slightly older girl is clutching a handful of hyacinths, skunk cabbage and daffodils – a harbinger of Easter.

Left: Japanese plum blossoms rain down onto the artesian spring where watercress and hardy violets grow.

Right: A skunk cabbage bloom is reflected in the artesian spring.

I am nearing the bank that overlooks the estuary and turn back to a small cut in the woods that returns to the creek. I hunch under fallen logs and straddle others on this delicate trail that has yet to be overrun by walkers. I find a trickle of a stream emptying into the Inlet: two four-foot-long metal cylinders are wedged across it. The cylinders look new but they are embossed with bead-like shapes around the ends and down one side. This identifies them as objects from another era – today, hot water tanks would be unembellished. On the south-facing bank leading to the old tanks is a drift of fawn lilies. Some are already opening, with their six-pointed starflowers nodding shyly earthwards. Fawn lilies are protected and can't be transplanted. Their tiny bulbs are set deep in the earth, and any disturbance usually kills them. These lilies will be blooming if they are at least seven years old, but others will emerge only as leopard-skin leaves springing out of the moss. The most impressive floral display occurs in late April and early May, when the slopes between the main trail and the stream resemble an English country garden. Exuberant trilliums push their way through salal, ferns and Oregon grape creating a tapestry of white, pink and maroon, each blossom framed by three deeply veined leaves. These colour variations are all of the same species. The darker shades indicate to insect pollinators that they should

Right: Hardy violets.

Facing page: Trilliums display their various colour stages.

concentrate their efforts on the unfertilized white blooms.

I'm stooped over as I make my way back on this narrow trail, trying not to slip, but at the same time to leave no trace of my footsteps. I turn in to the underbrush, which is supported by a massive shell midden, and just as I am about to emerge, I see a small iron shape hidden in the winter deadfall. It is a pair of shears, the wooden handles long gone. Perhaps they belonged to one of Jenny Butchart's gardeners or, more likely, one of the residents of the village who lived here in the 1940s or '50s. Beside them, appropriately, is a very early pop bottle. It has a frosty, light green exterior and proclaims itself a "delightful beverage made from the best ingredients." Stacked nearby are concrete bricks that look like short two-by-fours on the ground. They are three-quarters of an inch thick, one foot long and four inches wide, an elegant brick for some specific purpose. Historical finds are often revealed in early spring. Winter brings cold, wet and occasionally a blanket of snow, but by March the underbrush has been flattened and the spring winds have dried it. The lay of the land becomes visible for a short time, and some of its history lies exposed. Within a month the maple trees will sprout buds and the leaves will unfurl to an incredible ten to twelve inches across. Vistas that could be seen in February and March will be obstructed as the deciduous trees reassert themselves.

Near a crumbling foundation, a shiny chestnut is embedded in the intense green moss. I pick it up, thinking it might make a good worry stone, but it has a green

tail. Slowly, inexorably once started, it may become a chestnut tree one day. I place it back in its snug bed. It has fallen from one of Michael Rice's chestnut trees, which he planted here in the 1940s. They can be seen, three in a row, about 20 feet from the foundation of the Rice family home. Evelyn and Michael Rice raised their children here in one of the 13 houses that comprised Tod Village. Other village families of this era included the Hunters, O'Neils, Fergusons, McAlpines, Dyottes, Budinskis and Carriers. Michael Rice's daughter, Kathleen, told me a story of coming home from basketball practice in the dark, walking from Brentwood Village to Tod Village, and hearing the roar of lions not far away.

These were African lions, not cougars. From the 1950s to the 1970s, Rudy Bauersachs kept a rough zoo near Durrance Lake, just above Tod Inlet. I remember my father taking me to Rudy's Pet Park Zoo and seeing the massive wolf that paced its enclosure constantly. Kathleen reminisced about the times she and other children played in the flying saucers – the rotary kilns of the cement factory. She took me to a place in the woods where Mr. Cecil lived. He was the herdsman for Mr. and Mrs. Butchart, keeping livestock here for their family.

Yesterday I noticed a narrow, well-trodden track leading up the hill from the main pathway and decided to explore it. Dusk was falling, but I ventured forth and was rewarded with shooting stars and, even more exciting, lady's slippers. I hadn't seen them anywhere else in the park.

Today, with camera equipment, I decide to track them down again. The day has dawned clear with a few billowy clouds, but by noon the ground is carpeted with chunks of hail, and slate walls move across the sky. I suit up in my rain gear, but hope this weather system will pass. Rain begins to fall and then a sharp crack and a roll of thunder signal that the weather means business. The heavy, wet foliage narrows paths, and I decide to wait until tomorrow to photograph the lady's slippers.

After protecting my cameras from the now aggressive rain, I feel quite at home and wander back down the main trail savouring the dark, glistening forest. On a whim I turn in on an old trail, not intending to go far. Twenty-five years ago I took this trail, camera in hand,

Broad-leaved shooting stars grow in Garry oak meadows where the ground is wet in spring and dry in summer.

and came face to face with a saw-whet owl. I was 30 feet from it and couldn't believe my luck. I hardly breathed. I had a regular lens on my camera and wanted to change it for a longer lens, but was afraid the owl would be spooked, so I took a few tentative shots. The only reaction was the occasional lifting of an eyelid. "Well, what have I got to lose?" I thought, as I brought my other lens out and mounted it on the camera. I took several more shots, and still the owl remained immobile. Finally I advanced one pace too many. He lifted his wings and flew quietly away. At home, I scanned one of my reference books only to find what any seasoned birder would know: saw-whet owls have a reputation for appearing unruffled by humans. The joke was on me. But their reputation for being tame is a human perception – like rabbits, their defence if discovered is to remain still.

I return the next day to photograph the *Calypso bulbosa*. This entails lying on my stomach in the moss and twigs, as these delicate orchids are five to six inches tall and need to be photographed from below to view the droopy flower sac, the focus of interest. I feel like Gulliver in the land of the little people. Some of the lady's slippers are deep pink and others are pale. Like the fawn lilies and the trilliums, these are all the same species and should never be picked, as they grow in symbiosis with certain soil fungi; their environment can't be replicated in a domestic garden. But unlike the trilliums and fawn lilies, these little beauties have no nectar, and it is only the inexperienced bee that visits them.

I'm tired after crawling around, focusing intently on the lady's slippers, and I sit up to take a breath. My gear is strewn around me: tripods, backpack, cameras, lenses. How often do I just sit? I'm surrounded by a classic Vancouver Island Garry oak meadow. I breathe deeply and gaze absent-mindedly at the ground. Beside me are the tiniest of blue flowers, so small that a walker would find them difficult to spot: blue-eyed Marys. Just a short distance away is a slender purple flower: a lonely camas, a staple food of the Coast Salish for thousands of years. I'm off again, stretched out on the ground, turning the focus ring.

Once more I attempt to sit but catch a blur of motion to my right. A leaf in the breeze? I creep over and focus through a thatch of twigs to see a tree frog looking apprehensively back at me. He is about half a thumb long, lime green with orange markings. His camouflage is complete as he nestles in the green moss and last year's orange maple leaves. A sow bug travels by – hard worker of the woodland. I turn the close-up lens but a twig is in the way, and as soon as I move it he curls reflexively into an armoured ball. How can we walk in the forest without disrupting or killing the delicate inhabitants of the forest floor? I'm thankful that nature is so resilient.

I sit.

Facing page: The *Calypso bulbosa* has many names, including lady's slipper, fairy slipper, deer-head orchid and venus slipper.

Pages 50–52: Rare Chocolate lilies. Vanilla leaf. Nootka rose.

··· S U M M E R ···

N SUMMER, NATURE IS COMPLACENT, full of herself. There are no maples turning gold in the slanting sun, no powdery white landscapes for a day or two, no excitement of new growth as leaves and flowers unfurl during the daily changes of spring. The lush growth is at its apex; historical treasures are buried in the carpeted ground. Narrow pathways become impassable and the main thoroughfare in from Wallace Drive is wide and trampled down to its bare bones. Doggie bags litter the park. But of course my ambivalence about summer at Tod Inlet has less to do with the season than with the fact that I have to share the park with so many others at this time of the year.

Summer brings walkers and their dogs, mothers with baby carriages, cyclists and occasionally horseback riders – each person enjoying a respite from traffic, daily chores and to-do lists. The Inlet becomes a parking lot for sailboats, cruisers and the occasional yacht. Kayakers, rowers and canoeists glide over the water, and the purple martins rise up like bats from their nest boxes each time a boat of any description strays too close to the pilings they call home. Sticks are tossed to dogs, and children dip lines from the dock, occasionally depositing their wriggling catch into a jar of water for inspection. People visit the Nature Float and learn more about the natural, industrial and Native history of this place. First Nations volunteers, working with SeaChange, run the Nature Float.

Nikki Wright began SeaChange, a non-profit organization with a mandate to revitalize marine environments, in 1998. As a scientific diver she was concerned by what she saw on the Inlet's floor: it was a wasteland. A healthy Tod Inlet would have included a mass of nutrient-rich eelgrass growing from the seabed. These eelgrass meadows are the nurseries of the oceans and are at risk all along our coastal estuaries. Small crustaceans feed on the algae growing on the blades of grass, and in turn the crustaceans provide food for salmon as they enter the sea for the first time from their freshwater streams. The meadows also provide a safe haven from predation for many species, and new research has discovered that eelgrass has a profound role in controlling carbon in our atmosphere. Eelgrass meadows are able to store carbon 90 times more efficiently than an equivalent area of forest, embedding it in sediments, where it remains stable for thousands of years. SeaChange has planted 150,000 square feet of eelgrass in the Saanich

70

Inlet (including Tod Inlet), but nature's capacity to recover is still challenged by our modern habits. Environmental hazards leaching into these inlets include metals, pesticides, fungicides, fertilizers, animal and human waste, detergents, industrial waste and pharmaceuticals. Anchor-dragging by recreational boaters also uproots the eelgrass meadows, and there are designated areas where anchoring is not permitted.

The Saanich Inlet Protection Society (SIPS), founded by Frances Pugh, installed the Nature Float, the dock and gangway at Tod Inlet. The dock allows boaters to come ashore in their tenders without scouring the foreshore. Another SIPS improvement is *Pumpty Dumpty*, a boat that cruises Tod Inlet, Brentwood Bay and Saanich Inlet pumping effluent from recreational boats. In the United States, marinas are subsidized to provide this service, but no such liaison exists in Canada, and discharging effluent into our waters has been legal (except in marine parks) until recently. SIPS is a nonprofit society, spending $35,000 a year on this service while collecting about $1,000 in donations. The society was formed with the intention of gaining a marine park designation for Saanich Inlet, but so far this goal has not been realized.

As a true fjord, Saanich Inlet is very deep (700 feet at its deepest). A sill built up at its mouth prevents it from flushing its contents as the open sea does. For most of the year it is anoxic, meaning that the water contains very little dissolved oxygen. In the fall, new, oxygen-rich water surges over the sill and mixes with the oxygen-starved

Nikki Wright (*centre*) and John Bradley (*right*) and two SeaChange volunteers examine some of the Inlet's sea life.

water of the Inlet. This was not a problem when the Inlet was in its pristine state and the organisms living in its depths were adapted to these conditions. But when tons of toxic effluents are added to this somewhat static environment, the results can be lethal to an ecosystem. The marine environment at Tod Inlet was initially undermined by the cement plant, but in retrospect, this degradation might have been less harmful than the toxins unleashed by agriculture and development in the past 60 years. Tod Inlet curves off the larger Saanich Inlet like a relaxed forefinger, and the two fjords face similar challenges.

72

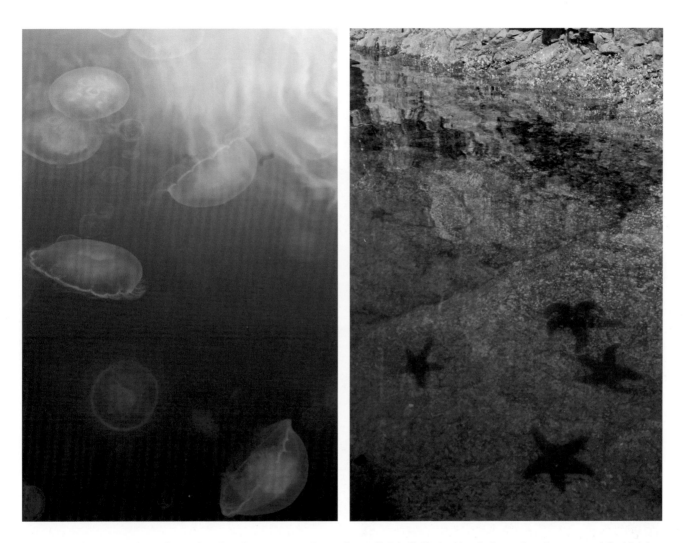

Tod Inlet looks pristine from the surface but the presence of countless jellyfish (*left*) signal a challenged environment while (*right*) starfish are diminishing.

74

Facing page: The boatways, and (*above*) the wharf site of the Tod Inlet Power Boaters' Association (1946 to 1981).

In 1946 local boat owners formed the Tod Inlet Power Boaters' Association. Many families in the area have fond memories of summers spent on the Inlet, and apparently John Wayne moored his 90-foot torpedo boat at the Inlet's mouth more than once.

John Grey remembers some of the characters who enjoyed the boating association and the lazy summers spent there when he was a youth 50 years ago. He tells of Dr. Bill Youlden, who moored his boat at Tod Inlet from the 1940s to the 1970s. His boat, *The Kangaroo*, was set up for his dental practice and he serviced Native and non-Native villages along the coast of Vancouver Island. A foot treadle operated his drill, and John remembers needing more than one appointment just to have a single tooth drilled (without anaesthetics) as the dentist and John's father would get carried away talking about fishing and other interests. Another character built a boat at the Inlet even though he was blind – apparently every plank was perfectly planed and fit so snugly that no caulking was needed, but it had no curving lines. A boater in his father's group was well known for his rabbit stew, which, accompanied by a bottle of beer and a swim, made for a perfect evening.

On March 31, 1981, the 35-year-old boaters' association was told that all boats would have to be relocated, as Tod Inlet had been sold to local developer Sam Bawlf. Before Bawlf's ownership, Ocean Cement and BC Cement, under their parent company, Genstar, had owned the land for decades. The Tod Inlet Boaters' Association was the custodian for Genstar, tending the facilities adjacent to their dock and boatways. Genstar had sold its holdings after two unsuccessful attempts to develop the property. In 1975 their first proposal included seven or eight neighbourhoods with a total population of three thousand, a 150-berth marina, houses, shops, two high-rise apartment complexes of 250 units each and a dike across the Inlet to provide road access. The land was designated commercial/recreational but Genstar was seeking rezoning to allow a residential component. In 1978 Ian Ross, the owner of Butchart Gardens, made a passionate speech at a Central Saanich Council meeting hoping to disallow any construction on the boundary his property shared with Genstar. In 1979 the council completed its Official Community Plan, making it even less likely that Genstar would be successful in rezoning the Inlet. The company cried foul, charged the council with procedural irregularities, and sold to Sam Bawlf. Bawlf made his bid to council that same year: a family vacation resort with a golf course, indoor/outdoor swimming pools, a performing arts centre and a marina. Stage two included a conference/resort hotel and a fitness spa.

Phillip Paul, an activist and leader from the Tsartlip Band, spoke out against the Bawlf proposal, arguing that development would destroy the fisheries promised to the Saanich First Nations by the treaties signed by James Douglas, governor of the colony of Vancouver Island, and Saanich chiefs in 1852. In a 36-page document presented to the Central Saanich Council, he also cited the spiritual values of S̲NIT¢EȽ, their former winter village, and its continuing importance to the Saanich people.

The midden site at the estuary of the creek is one of three at Tod Inlet, indicating where the W̱SÁNEĆ people lived for centuries.

Ian Ross and Phillip Paul were high-profile individuals in the community, but they were not the only opposing voices. As the news got out, each time a developer made a new proposal, bigger halls had to be rented, as the council chambers proved inadequate for the numbers of people showing up at meetings.

Bawlf went into partnership with Vancouver magnate Murray Pezim, and their combined vision included the original resort plan, but also high-tech industry much like the newly successful Silicon Valley in California. When it became evident that the proposal would not be easily passed, Pezim decided to sell, and FAMA Holdings (owned by King Faisal of Saudi Arabia) became the new owner. It purchased the land for $7.2-million, and this final proposal for Tod Inlet included a townsite of eight thousand people. When confronted by opposition, an exasperated FAMA Holdings spokesperson said, "Tod Inlet is a sick piece of land already despoiled by cement plants, chemical labs, quarries and decaying structures." She was right, of course, but the opposition only increased.

76

Earl Claxton smokes salmon for Parks Day at the Inlet. Claxton, a member of the Tsawout Band, teaches ethnobotany in the school system.

Above: An otter devours a giant Pacific octopus, a highly intelligent creature with a life span of only four years.

Facing page: While canoeing on Tod Inlet I surprised an otter eating an octopus. He slipped into the water, allowing me to photograph his prey.

A pivotal group to speak out and foster research for the preservation of Tod Inlet was Citizens Action to Save the Environment Society (CASE), started in Victoria in 1972 by Gwen and Derrick Mallard. Gwen had founded the Society for Promoting Environmental Conservation (SPEC), one of Canada's first citizens' advocacy groups, in Coquitlam in 1968. Her first task was to take on industries that were polluting the Fraser River. A year later she went up against Kaiser Resources to protest their coal strip-mining in the East Kootenays' Elk Valley, the winter habitat of herds of elk. This very influential activist was known to many of us in the late 1970s as the quietly dignified, grey-haired woman who served us wholesome soup and sandwiches at Gwen's Café on West Saanich Road. In the 1980s Gwen Mallard worked with the Tsartlip First Nation to protect Tod Inlet. Concurrently, CASE fostered studies on every aspect of the Inlet, including David Gray's extensive research on the history of the Vancouver Portland Cement Company. Ron dePol, who spent four years working to reintroduce salmon to Tod Creek, also spoke out, while Dr. Grant Keddie and Dr. Richard Hebda from the Royal British Columbia Museum drew attention to the prehistoric First Nations sites and the need for more documentation before anything went forward. Archaeological surveys were done in 1982, 1991 and 1993.

Tod Inlet had weathered the cement factory, pollution from the surrounding lands, and a succession of would-be developers in the twentieth century. Its fate was finally decided when Moe Sihota, as Minister of

The purple martin nest boxes atop the cedar pilings come alive in summer. This successful colony is the fourth largest in BC. The nest box program began after only five to six pairs of purple martins were thought to exist in BC in the 1950s. John Creviston has been cleaning and building the boxes for a decade now, and each summer he and volunteers band 130 to 140 new chicks. These large swallows fly from South America to breed at Tod Inlet.

Environment, Lands and Parks for the provincial government, created Gowlland Tod Provincial Park in 1995 as part of a Commonwealth Heritage Legacy Program conceived by local and provincial governments, organizations and businesses in the wake of the 1994 Commonwealth Games held in Victoria. It should be noted, however, that the First Nations community does not consider that this land has been ceded to the province.

The mandate for Gowlland Tod Provincial Park is primarily conservation, with recreation secondary. It is never to be promoted as a recreational destination, and management's focus is on protecting natural ecosystems, biodiversity and archaeological and cultural values. The original plan emphasizes continuing involvement with First Nations in planning and managing the park.

84

Facing page: The dam built by the Vancouver Portland Cement Company in 1917.

Right: The remains of a century-old water system and other industrial debris still clog the creek at the base of the dam.

IT IS A HOT AUGUST AFTERNOON but the entrance to the park promises a welcome relief. Only steps down the path, the thick overhead canopy creates a drop in temperature similar to the experience of entering a stone church. I walk onto the streambed just below the dam. A gentle trickle, reminiscent of a backyard water feature, splashes down its concrete face. In winter and spring I would be pushed off my feet by the force of the water, but now there is only a still pool of reddish water where mosquitoes are hatching. I stand on an exposed concrete structure that may have encased the water pipe to the former village and factory site. Many other century-old remnants lie permanently sunken into the streambed – heavy, uncompromising and intrusive. There is no room even for an ingenious salmon to spawn or a trout to make its way back upstream, but this is two months before spawning time and water conditions would be different by then.

I follow Tod Creek downstream, jumping from one rock outcropping to the next, enjoying the mysterious bottom, now naked to the light of day. The boulders and bedrock are covered with a fine, hardy moss, ancient bracken ferns and tiny stinging nettles, creating a fresh environment after the violence of the winter waters. Although the water gets low, the creek never dries up. The drainage from Prospect Lake ensures a constant flow that has made Tod Creek a viable stream for fish in the past. Until the mid-twentieth century, chum, spring and coho salmon and cutthroat trout made their journeys back to their ancestral spawning grounds here. The Friends of Tod Creek Watershed (FTCW), founded by Mary Haig-Brown in 1999, have been researching ways to revitalize the watershed that feeds Tod Creek. This area includes 21 kilometres of watercourses, 29 known wetlands, numerous ponds and five lakes.

It is a complex issue. Just south of the park entrance, behind the Red Barn Market on West Saanich Road, is an area that stays flooded for about ten months of the year, Tod Flats. As early as 1860 the flats were drained by digging a ditch along the west side in order to farm it. Prior to that, Tod Creek meandered through a wetland that included willow, dogwood and crabapple, a natural harvestland of wildfowl and plants for the Native population. It was farmed, complete with agricultural chemicals, until recently. FTCW has drawn up a comprehensive proposal to return Tod Flats to its original state so that water may be purified naturally and levels can be sustained for fish enhancement in Tod Creek. In anticipation of a revitalized Tod Creek, Butchart Gardens has agreed in principle to install a fish ladder around the dam that was built on the creek in 1917.

Right: The phantom orchid is extremely rare and grows and reproduces in much the same way Indian pipe does, although it has a preference for soils containing limestone. In Canada these orchids are found only sporadically in southern BC and may go dormant for many years if conditions aren't perfect. Even a footstep too close to a phantom orchid's roots can compact the soil and lessen its chances for survival.

Facing page: Indian pipe is an ancient plant that co-existed with the dinosaurs. Although its whiteness indicates that it lacks chlorophyll, it is not a fungus. It grows near a tree root in decaying plant material. Its main food is the fungus *Russula*, a mycorrhizal which in turn is fed by the nearby tree. Indian pipe has tiny flowers that are pollinated by equally small bees.

The honeybee is dying at alarming rates worldwide due to the use of pesticides (neonicotinoids).

The pale swallowtail butterfly (*above*) is hopefully doing better than the monarch butterfly, which used to be a common sight here in summer. Its population has diminished by 85 per cent in the last 15 years due to habitat loss and the eradication of its necessary food, the milkweed.

Facing page: Although the wild sweet pea and morning glory (*lower left and right*) are considered invasives, the harebells and daisies (*upper left*) are indigenous wildflowers. The *Penstemon* (*upper right*) has 116 wild varieties in the Pacific Northwest.

In the late 1970s, Ron dePol wondered about the viability of the stream across the road from his house, little more than a ditch on its way to Tod Inlet. His walks took him above Tod Inlet to two lakes whose creeks eventually flowed into Tod Creek. dePol had noticed that Heal Lake Creek was foul, while Durrance Lake Creek seemed pure. He placed live fish in the various streams and watched the results. In Heal Creek and Tod Creek the fish died, but they remained healthy in Durrance Creek as long as they were able to stay there. Obviously, Heal Creek, which captured effluent from the Hartland Landfill, Victoria's garbage dump, was the polluting source.

Ron dePol teamed up with his friend Dr. Lorne Ebell, who had retired from the BC Ministry of Forests and had been involved in rehabilitating other streams on Vancouver Island. In 1983 they formed the Tod Creek Water Enhancement Society and wrote letters to the Capital Regional District (CRD) outlining what they had discovered regarding the landfill and its impact on the streams in the area. The CRD was running out of space at the Hartland Landfill and was entertaining the idea of emptying nearby five-acre Heal Lake and filling it with garbage. An alternative plan was to use Heal Lake as the new aerating pool, replacing the existing one at the dumpsite, which was a foaming black pool that stank of mysterious leachate and was basically uncontained. It was a lose-lose situation for Heal Lake, a lake that had apparently been left off the official map in Vancouver, further sealing its fate. (Dr. Richard Hebda of the Royal BC Museum had discovered mature trees in its basin and was able to take samples which gave clues to climate dating back 4,200 years.)

While the Hartland Landfill was experiencing these growing pains, Ebell and dePol got to work on the enhancement of Tod Creek. They spoke to every resident whose property abutted the creek, from Prospect Lake to Tod Inlet, stressing the need to keep pollutants from entering it. They planted over a thousand trees along the stream's edge (mostly along Wallace Drive) to keep the water cool and oxygenated for future fish. A few steep sections of the stream were blasted to ease the upstream journey, and toward the Inlet, where the stream flattened, boulders were moved to create parallel channels where the fish could rest. A federal youth program called Katimavik made it possible for many middle and high school students to be involved in the project. The lower trails beside the stream are the result of the hard work of these volunteers.

Facing page, left: A low Tod Creek reveals its grassy bottom and (*right*) trees are reflected where the stream joins the estuary.

Pages 92–93: In the 1980s paths near the streambed were built by students involved in the Katimavik program and volunteers moved boulders in the lower streambed to facilitate hoped-for future salmon runs.

In 1983 the society released 4,700 coho fry into Tod Creek, and two-and-a-half years later there was great excitement as eight coho returned to the creek to spawn. In the previous year an even healthier run of returning salmon were eaten by the resident seals. In response, Ebell and dePol found a net normally used to stop submarine torpedoes and strung it across the Inlet. dePol's son Chad, a diver, secured the net to the ocean floor. In 1986 their work paid off. They milked the two remaining females of their eggs, mixed them with the milt from the males, and headed to the Goldstream hatchery, where the young fry would be raised until it was time to reintroduce them to Tod Creek. The Tod Creek Water Enhancement Society volunteers worked steadily for four years, often putting in 40-hour weeks, but life had other plans for these two environmentalists and their families. The Ebells began an organic farm near Duncan and the dePols opened Russell Books in Victoria. Their initial ten-year plan for Tod Creek was shortened, but they did make some positive changes to both the creek and parts of the watershed. Sadly, though, the reintroduction of salmon remains an uphill battle. Heal Lake was drained in 1991 and filled with garbage. The runoff from the landfill was still leaching into the streams without being screened or diluted, so a pipe was installed and the toxic mix was routed through the sewer system, where it eventually found its way to the MacCaulay Point outfall and Juan de Fuca Strait.

I PAUSE TO TAKE A PHOTO of several logs stacked up in the stream. As I frame the shot I notice a movement on one of the logs. A mink is staring at me, frozen for a moment, halfway across a big downed fir. I snap a couple of shots and he turns, humps his way back to the opposite shore, works his way downstream under the fringe of swordferns that line the creek and vanishes. I wonder what this mink is finding to eat here. Its preferred food would be small fish and crustaceans, but this is not nineteenth-century Tod Creek. Apparently minks are incredibly versatile in their eating habits: crabs, crayfish, insects, birds, ducklings, voles, mice, shrews, lizards, muskrats, frogs and snakes are also fair game.

I often look at the latticework of fallen trees choking the stream and imagine cleaning it up. But this messy habitat, along with the canopy of live trees, is just as crucial for the mink as it would be for the salmon. The living trees keep the water temperature cool in summer, thereby supporting all that thrives in the stream. The larger dead trees provide hollows where the female minks make their dens. The dense foliage and thick logjams also provide cover for these shy creatures whose predator, the great grey owl, glides silently through the forest.

94

Outside the park the maples are tinged with gold, even though it is only the first week of September. Inside the park, under the damp, dense canopy, they still retain their vibrant, deep lime-green hue. Green saturates my vision: from fern fronds to treetops, I'm enveloped in a monochromatic world from which other colours have been banished. Only a few weeks ago I was able to dance my way down the middle of the streambed, hopping from one mossy granite protrusion to the next. Now, after only a day's rainfall, the tiny rivulets have become pools again and the rocky outcrops are shrinking in size. But the creek's delicate murmur is still magical and I'll miss it once the winter rains have transformed it into a noisy torrent.

At this end of summer all the trails and stream banks show the wear of hundreds of visitors. Paths that were smooth clay are now inches deeper with stones unearthed and jutting up. Rambunctious dogs have turned creekside fern banks into muddy hollows. But as chaotic and trampled as things may seem now, Mother Nature has a way of constantly renewing and reclaiming herself.

Right: Salal flowers (*top*), Snowberry (*below*).

Facing page: Huckleberry.

Pages 98-99: The *Jennie B*, an electric boat, takes Butchart Gardens visitors on a tour of Tod Inlet. A kayaker heads for the mouth of Tod Inlet where purple starfish dot the rock ledges.

··· F A L L ···

THE SKY IS A WELCOME CLEAR BLUE and the air is warm as I reach the entrance to the park, but only a few feet along the path the light dims and a dampness seeps into my body. We've had a couple of all-night rains this week, and the creek is rushing to the sea with new intensity, replacing the lilting sound of the summer creek with the roar of winter as the water begins to rise. The low afternoon sun slants through the tall Douglas firs on the opposite bank and I'm blinded each time the sun shoots a beam between the trunks. Moisture is evaporating from the trees nearest me, sending curling wisps of fog into the air, incandescent against the sunlight.

I follow a narrow deer trail, noticing the glistening chocolate beads of recent droppings. This unused part of the park is their refuge. Beside the trail lie the white bones of a deer where it bedded down for the last time. I've reached a tiny Garry oak rock outcropping with a beam of sunlight illuminating a mossy knob. The musty odour of oak leaves hangs in the fall air. I sit and gaze at the thick green moss that seems to be sprouting new shoots even in this season, and I marvel at a tiny fir seedling nestled there that mimics the structure of the moss sprouts. Beside me is a slender bone. I twirl it in my fingers. It is hollow, indicating an avian origin, and about three-eighths of an inch thick. My guess is it's a raven bone. The sun shifts from my rock perch, creating a subtle drop in temperature, and I instinctively rise, wanting to follow its warming rays.

Mushrooms are everywhere, cleaving the earth with their delicate but determined bodies. They are red, yellow, orange, translucent white, creamy white, brown, beige and even bright green – some are as large as side plates, others barely the size of a flaxseed. Each one transforms itself as it peaks in perfection and then decays, making identification difficult. It's easy to imagine that I'm looking at different types as down-turned caps become horizontal and then up-turned, a dull mushroom begins to shine, a white one becomes ochre, subterranean fungi explode from the moss and become orange, brain-like creatures or creamy, fluted chanterelles. The most unusual mushroom I've encountered is a type of fluted *Helvella*. The top looks like a mangled three-tailed hat of a court jester and the stalk is ribbed and traced with oblong holes. Even the colour of these four-inch-high mushrooms is difficult to describe: a kind of dusky mauve-brown which makes them very easy to miss, but as strange as I may find them, they seem quite common in this area. White stands out so vividly in the dark forest, and a stand of white fairy fingers or translucent jelly tooth mushrooms flash their presence even if I am not paying attention.

I look up from mushroom hunting and realize I'm at the estuary. All is quiet and the shallow water 20 feet below is clear. I spot a small log that seems to be moving; it's an otter swimming to the bank below me. The trees here are mostly alders, indicating an old clearing. I stop and search the forest floor without moving. I see a shard of white glass, pieces of tin, half a cylinder of ceramic tile and another cylinder of solid concrete that may have served as a foundation support. This is the edge of the former housing area for the Chinese workers of the cement plant and I decide to backtrack slightly to investigate this trace of a village. I don't expect to locate any treasures but am amazed at what I do find. Every footfall bears witness to this small community's existence. There are several holes dug in the ground, four feet deep and almost as wide. An outhouse? A root cellar? I step gingerly, hunching under long branches of ocean spray, but my boots slip on the thick green shards of ancient beer bottles, my ankle turns on a camouflaged brick and I look up just in time to find that a branch across my path is actually a length of rebar. Metal fencing wire, heavy

Right: *Helvella* mushroom (*top*), Lobster mushroom (*below*).

Facing page: The *Hygrocybe psittacinus*, or parrot mushroom, will soon fade to a tawny-pink colour, making identification difficult later in the season.

iron struts, wire mesh, tin roofing, even crockery peek through the forest debris. As I skulk, I'm constantly stepping on the rusting corrugated roofing buried under the leaves: it prangs and crackles, making disconcerting sounds in the otherwise quiet forest. I'm shocked to find a glazed ceramic bowl and a pig bone. Did Yat Tong eat a meal from this bowl? It has been said that he was the only one who knew how to make the flowerpots properly when the cement plant became a tile and pot factory, in business until the 1950s.

Yat Tong is one of the most memorable of all the Chinese workers, having spent about 50 years at Tod Inlet. He arrived in Canada in 1912 aboard a ship that was supplying construction workers for the Canadian Pacific Railway. No doubt becoming appalled at the number of his fellow countrymen who were dying on the railway, he made his way westward and somehow landed at Tod Inlet working for the Vancouver Portland Cement Company. After the close of the company in 1921, he stayed on and worked with Dem Carrier, the village superintendent, and others in a scaled-down operation that manufactured tiles. He spent his final years working for Jennie Butchart as a gardener and was still living in an old cabin in the Chinese village as late as the 1960s.

The Vancouver Portland Cement Company employed almost 200 Chinese men in the factory's early years and gradually tapered to a steady crew of about 80. These men built their own buildings, probably with lumber offered by the cement company. The area above the estuary, where I'm standing now, had a semicircle of four cabins and a communal cook shack. A large dormitory was built farther away in the clearing where a small concrete structure still stands – the last remaining building from the cement plant days.

It would have been a grim life for these Chinese workers, but hardly different from the plight of most immigrant workers in Canada at this time. They worked long hours for low wages and fended for themselves domestically: raising livestock, growing vegetables, cooking and doing the laundry in this bachelor's village. Tuberculosis was common in this dusty, gritty environment, and diseases spread quickly due to crowded living quarters and lack of proper sanitation.

Some of the workers' social outlets may have included playing games such as mahjong and fan-tan, or indulging in an opium pipe or beer procured from Victoria's Chinatown (the oldest in Canada). But as isolated as they were at Tod Inlet, some respite could be had if they managed to travel to the city: the inter-urban electric rail line stopped at Lime Kiln Road (today's Benvenuto Road). In Victoria they may have made contact with friends from their home province, attended a funeral, gambled the evening away, had a familiar meal at one of the many restaurants, sent news or money home, picked up mail or even visited a brothel.

Facing page (left and clockwise): Part of a wood stove and crockery, a glazed bowl and pig bone, and pieces of Chinese beer bottles.

Facing page: The last remaining building of the Vancouver Portland Cement Company, situated where the men's bunkhouses once stood.

Above: At the site of the former stable, built almost entirely of concrete, sit these long, awl-like pieces of equipment. They were likely screw conveyors used to move clay.

From 1900 to 1910 Victoria was home to the largest Chinatown in North America. In 1911 the Chinese of Victoria numbered 3,458 – about half the population of the city at that time, and their town covered six blocks. Little Guangzhou, as it was known, was anything but a shantytown. Well-heeled merchants and their families owned dry goods, grocery and produce stores. There were tailors, herbalists, teahouses, gaming rooms and joss houses (Chinese temples). An impressive cemetery was established at Harling Point in 1903, and in 1909 the Chinese community built its own school, where Chinese and English were taught, as Chinese children were not allowed to attend the colonial schools.

The European families who lived at Tod Inlet did interact with some of the Chinese workers, and relations seemed fairly cordial. Mary Parsell, who raised a family here, spoke of the kindness of the Chinese cook, Mr. Losee, whenever she was in need. She was unused to getting provisions only monthly and often ran short. (In the first seven years of the cement factory, the only way to transport quantities of goods to Tod Village was by ship, as there was no proper road and the interurban rail line only lasted from 1910–1921.) On occasion Mr. Losee would give Parsell a much-coveted loaf of bread that was intended for the workers he had to feed. The families asked permission to use the communal dining room in the workers' cookhouse for special occasions and were often presented with a cake from the same busy cook. The Parsell family, in turn, hosted English classes for the workers at their house. But Mary Parsell's son, Norm, remembered children throwing snowballs and rocks at the Chinese workers and occasionally yanking on their long pigtails, although the workers made no move to retaliate. This small village, although not ideal, was unique due to the close proximity of the two communities. In other areas, such as Vancouver, racial tensions were rising and riots were evidence of the animosity felt for the Chinese.

In 1906, 40 Sikhs came to work at the Vancouver Portland Cement plant. Living conditions were as basic for the Sikh workers as they were for the Chinese, but the isolation must have been even more acute, as no established Sikh community existed for these men. In the early years of the plant the Sikhs were the stokers and firemen. Each time the bricks in a kiln became exhausted, the stokers had to replace them. The old bricks were tossed into the water and can still be seen on the shore adjacent to the stacks of unused concrete pilings. After discarding these firebricks, the men entered the still-warm kilns to reline them, using pieces of lumber strapped to their feet for protection. The rotary kilns were thick steel tubes, seven feet in diameter and 70 feet long, and were heated to a temperature of 2700 degrees Fahrenheit in order to fuse the powdered limestone and clay. It must have taken many hours for the bricks to cool, and production time was lost until the kilns could be relined. By 1910 these Sikh workers had all moved on after witnessing the deaths of Chinese workers due to tuberculosis caused by dust and typhus carried by lice in overcrowded living quarters. But the death

of one of their countrymen was probably a deciding factor. Tar Gool Singh had caught a cold that developed into consumption, no doubt exacerbated by his living and working conditions. When the cement plant owners discovered his plight they offered to pay for his stay at St. Joseph's Hospital, but he refused, as eating from the plates of white people would cause him to lose his Punjabi caste. When he was close to death he was taken to the hospital, but his co-workers and a brother wanted to cremate him on a traditional funeral pyre and send a bone back to India to cast into the Ganges to ensure his passage to paradise. A large wooden pyre was built in the forest at Tod Inlet, and on an April morning Tar Gool Singh's last rites were honoured. The descendants of many of these men live in the Victoria area. Some family names include Wirk, Singh, Johal, Dhillon and Jawl.

I CROSS TWO WOODEN FOOTBRIDGES and saunter past three chestnut trees. A winter wren gives a quick chirp as it vacates the steps I'm moving towards. It hops only a few feet away, foraging intently on the ground. A frog croaks, his voice conjuring up images of the huge species that has been introduced to Vancouver Island, but I recognize it as our tiny indigenous tree frog. I arrive at the sunny, open space where the men's bunkhouse was built into the hillside facing the Inlet. A huge old maple tree dominates this area, its lumpy trunk mostly burls. A First Nations couple is walking in front of me and I watch as the young man points to the big maple. He is showing his girlfriend the image of Snoopy

embedded in the gnarly bark of the ancient tree. The cartoon character is so obvious on first sight that the young girl says, "Did somebody do that?"

"No!" says the boyfriend, laughing, and they walk on.

I check to see how many boats are in the Inlet today and notice swirls of taupe-coloured marbling on the water. It looks toxic but I'm hoping it's some kind of natural algae bloom. The fast-flowing creek shows cause for concern as well: thick, creamy foam blobs the size of beach balls have built up at intervals along the surface of the water. I perch on one of the concrete walls by the old boatways to get a better vantage point to photograph the Inlet's strange surface. With a slip of my foot the earth gives way and tumbles into the sea. I scan the shoreline and realize that when I first began walking here about 30 years ago the shoreline extended 20 feet farther into the Inlet than it does today. The erosion is constantly exposing new structures and artifacts from the former factory. But this is only my limited perspective – more than a century ago, before the cement plant, the shoreline would have been many yards farther inland, and what I am witnessing is the erosion of an unnatural shoreline of concrete, metal and clinker.

Today I've come to the park in a troubled mood and I march down the path looking straight ahead, interiorized. I need the physical exertion of a good walk and care little for the glistening emerald green of salal and ferns that surround me. I nod hello to familiar walkers and attempt a smile. Before I know it, I've walked as far as I can and stop to stare across the narrow Inlet. A curve of a massive cedar tree is reflected, its doubled image creating a sweeping arc. I know it well and, like an old friend, it is just ... there. The forest reflects what it always has: an uncompromising timelessness. Melodrama has no place here.

I don't find serenity today, but I do find some perspective. How little it takes: just a walk in the woods. This is a landscape and seascape that has been strangled by the twentieth century's encroachments and still it offers sustenance. It is a healing place, as the W̱SÁNEĆ people know so well.

A small laminated message hanging from the park entrance sign reads: "Save Mary's Lake. Save it as a link between Gowlland Tod and Thetis parks. Buy a square metre for $10. If $4.2-million is not raised by January 22, this 107-acre parcel will not be saved but subdivided."

The groundswell of active conservationists in this province is unprecedented. We've had to abandon government as the logical planner, provider and conserver and form our own non-governmental organizations to sustain what we recognize as our life's blood. Volunteerism is a necessity, and thankfully many of us have the passion and the opportunity to donate our time or money for the preservation of parts of the planet. The inherent reverence and knowledge that First Nations people have had for the environment is being reborn.

Marbling on the Inlet near the dock.

Tod Inlet was the site of a traditional winter village for the W̱SÁNEĆ people, but it was used in the summer too as a place for clamming, catching grouse and gathering edible and medicinal plants.

The waving stands of eelgrass protected young salmon, but were also home to clams. Often the clams didn't dig themselves into the seabed, but hung from the eelgrass, making harvesting a simple procedure of picking them off. When digging was necessary, three-pronged forks were used. These were cut from the branches of the ocean spray bush, then steamed and bent into claws. The clams were dried in layers by the fire until they were rock hard and then strung into necklaces. These were considered a delicacy, and the Kelowna and Yakama people eagerly traded wool for these nutritious and portable candies.

The plentiful ocean spray had many uses – steeped in hot water, the dried flower heads produced a tea that treated diarrhea and could also prevent sickness due to blowflies. When it went to seed in the fall it was time to hunt deer, and its branches were used as arrows. These arrows were sometimes tipped with gold. When early colonizers discovered this, it set off a mini gold rush at the source – Goldstream. Ocean spray branches were also made into knitting needles and fish hooks.

The area around Tod Inlet provided many curative plant substances. Small nodules on Douglas firs contain pitch, readily available to heal cuts – the wound is knitted together by the pitch and cleansed by its antiseptic qualities; even scarring is minimized by a vitamin E-like

Ocean spray.

substance. Oregon grape berries were used as a remedy for shellfish poisoning, although the intervals between red tide occurrences in centuries past apparently were measured in generations rather than in years or months as they are today. Other infusions from this ubiquitous shrub assisted stroke victims or those with nerve damage.

I have been talking with John Bradley, and he gave me an almost stream-of-consciousness history lesson. He began volunteering with the Nature Float several years ago, liaising with SeaChange, and he also works with Dr. Nancy Turner, a leading authority on indigenous medicinal plants. Bradley's heritage is part Ditidaht and part W̱SÁNEĆ, and he has become an eloquent and knowledgeable interpreter for anyone interested in local

John Bradley gives a talk to park visitors outlining the many uses of local plants for the W̱SÁNEĆ people.

Native history and especially the cultural uses of the plants in the area. Bradley told me about the hunting technique used in the Place of the Blue Grouse: these hefty birds perch on high branches in the afternoon but gradually make their way down to the lower branches in the evening until they are within reach by nightfall. A well-aimed conk on the head by a hunter tumbled the unsuspecting bird into a basket.

The air is cold and humid and not many walkers are here on this late afternoon that threatens rain. As I pass near the outhouses I notice a young woman working in a cordoned-off area where there are new plantings. She is working with SeaChange to repatriate indigenous plants while eradicating such non-native species as blackberry, wild pea, ivy and columbine. She tells me about the new plantings of hairy honeysuckle, red alder, red flowering currant, Oregon grape, Garry oaks, saskatoon bushes and shooting stars. Camas and chocolate lilies will also be reintroduced but will take four years to flower. We talk about the tiny lizards that scurry around the warmed concrete foundations in summer, and I learn that these are invasive European wall lizards. We still have our native species, the northern alligator lizard, but the two species are very similar in size and colouring, and it takes an expert eye to tell them apart.

My conversation with her takes me back to a day many years earlier when I had just begun photographing the park. I was on the shore framing an image of clamshells packed into the dark earth of a midden. I caught a movement and quickly changed lenses. Luck-ily the indigenous alligator lizard froze, and I was able to capture his stunning little body as he stared back at me.

Our fixation to maintain indigenous species may seem extreme in some instances, but the alternative is equally extreme. How different is the desire to stop the destruction of an oil spill on the ocean from the desire to replace the smothering qualities of English ivy at Tod Inlet? However, as well-meaning as we are, our attempts to restore the interconnectedness of plants, animals, fish, water, insects, algae, fungi and even humans are clumsy at best compared to nature's intrinsic balancing act.

Facing page: Tod Inlet is a study in native and non-native plants. *Clockwise from upper left*: The Himalayan blackberry, although much loved for its fruit, is considered an invasive species, while the clematis, nicknamed "Old Man's Beard," is indigenous. St. John's wort, introduced to North America in the 1700s, has medicinal properties but is very adept at crowding out native plants. And a single apple clings to a branch in late November. Crabapple trees are native to this area, but this one was planted by an early Tod Inlet settler.

Pages 134-135: The indigenous alligator lizard, and to the right the second-largest slug in the world. The banana slug is an important part of the ecosystem, as it consumes matter from the forest floor and redeposits it as soil.

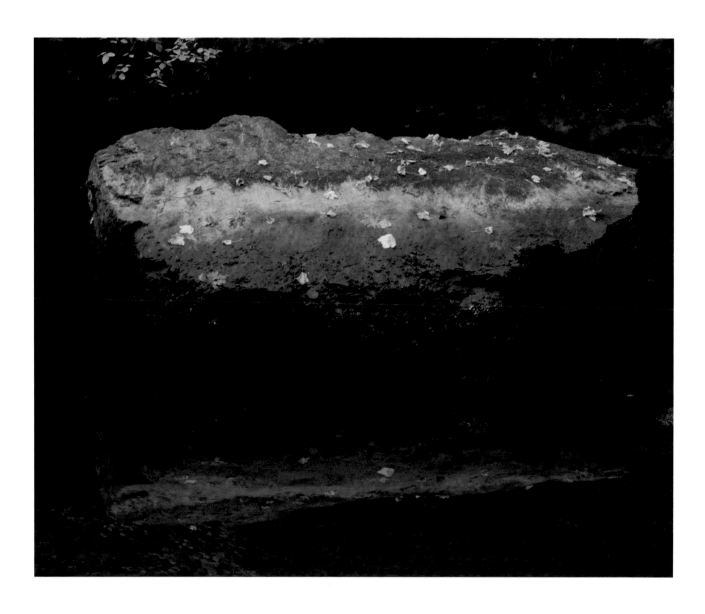

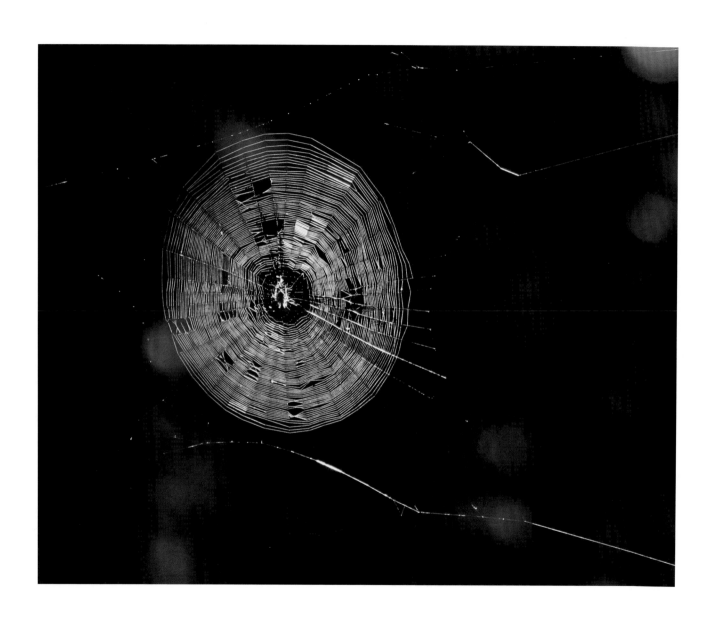

··· W I N T E R ···

DECOMPRESSION BEGINS as soon as I enter the trail to the park: traffic sounds are consumed by the dense vegetation, and the shushing sound of the stream becomes the new reality. My breath deepens, shoulders relax and my mind begins to receive instead of transmit.

I'm enveloped in the verdure of this mixed forest, even in December, as photosynthesis never stops on this coast. Only the maple and alder leaves are absent, allowing the weak light of the winter sky to penetrate the forest canopy. As I near the estuary, I turn south down a trail bordered by several gnarled apple trees. Firs and cedars block my view of the Inlet, and I have to duck under them at an old house foundation before I get a glimpse of the sea. It is three o'clock on a cloudy December afternoon and the sun is dropping behind the wall of firs on the opposite shore. Darkness is a couple of hours away, and Joylorn Creek, invisible on the far shore, empties into Tod Inlet with the kind of hypnotic sound any new-age musician would die for. Crows twist across the Inlet, heading for their nocturnal roosts, and a drake mallard barks, injecting a comical note into the mix.

I turn from the shore and prop my camera gear against the concrete remnants of this former Tod Village house, sitting only 15 feet from the bank of the Inlet. Periwinkle (the smaller *Vinca minor*) hugs the foundation and covers the ground; only the well-trodden paths have beaten it back as if a gardener had edged them. The coarse Portland cement on the exterior of the three-foot-high foundation has been scored to look like large bricks: we imitate the past until the future takes over. Stones are embedded in the outside walls, but the inside walls are smooth. Three concrete washtubs are built into the foundation, with angled fronts that once accommodated glass washboards.

Colourful graffiti is splashed across the interior walls of the foundation, creating a bizarre outdoor courtyard. An impressive cedar tree, surrounded by a concrete base, is situated where the front door and lawn would have been at the west side of the house.

154

This was once the home of James Reginald "Jim" Carrier, his wife, Evelyn May "Billie," and their family. Carrier arrived here shortly after the First World War and lived in the village for 30 years. During this time he held the positions of village superintendent, postmaster and head of the tile and pot manufacturing plant. Directly behind the former three-storey home is a tennis court. Few passersby would be aware of the court today, but two rusty pipes that supported the net are still standing. On the east side of the house, overlooking the Inlet, were terraced gardens and lawns. Up the hill from the terraces was a garage and above that the vegetable garden. The Carrier house also had a dock and a float that extended halfway across the Inlet.

One of the Carriers' children, Dem Carrier, was born here in 1925. He remembered when the British battleship *Exeter* was in Victoria and the officers came out, dressed in their whites, to play tennis at his family's home at Tod Inlet. He also told me about hunting grouse and deer at an early age and fishing for trout in Tod Creek. When Dem Carrier and his friends were about eleven years old, they devised a way for the salmon and trout to get past the dam on Tod Creek in the fall. Several old logs were laid in a shelf at the top of the dam. When the water was deep enough on the high side they took one log out and created a fall of water over the dam. The fish circled in the pool below the seven-foot concrete wall waiting for this much needed water to splash down. They wriggled their way up the wall, often making several attempts before reaching the creek above the dam.

When the dam was built in 1917 a fish ladder had been installed, but by the 1930s it was no longer viable. These young boys were all avid fishermen and understood the cycles of the fishes' life. Without permission from their elders, they invented their own solution.

Today I'm walking to the Inlet with Lorna Pugh, 92 years old and a daughter of the Thomson pioneers of the area, accompanied by her daughter Winona, who is a member of the Friends of Tod Creek Watershed. (Frances Pugh, the founder of SIPS, is another of her daughters). Even though Lorna lived in Brentwood Bay she has fond memories of Tod Village. "In the winter the Carriers would flood the tennis court and we'd skate here," she tells me. Her father, Lorne Thomson, was a teamster and also ran a farm. At the beginning of summer, Lorna and her father herded their cattle down to Tod Inlet to what is now the farthest point in the park, where the old bollard sits. Here, at the Inlet's narrowest point, Thomson walked his lead cow into the water and, with himself in a rowboat, swam the cattle to the steep shore on the opposite side. The cattle spent the summer above the Inlet, in the Durrance Lake area, reluctant to make the return trip home by water. In the fall the Thomsons coaxed them back to the farm, using the road this time.

The point of land where Lorne Thomson herded his cattle across the Inlet.

Lorna Kenyon was born at Tod Inlet in 1930 and moved with her family to Esquimalt when she was only three, but she tells me of her grandfather's history at the Inlet. Captain Oscar Scarfe ferried mail and people between Tod Inlet and Bamberton – the site of the new cement plant established by H.K.G. Bamber of London in 1919 after a shaky start due to the First World War. The Bamberton plant began full production in 1921 after Robert Butchart, Bamberton's new president and managing director, had shut down the Vancouver Portland Cement Company at Tod Inlet the same year. Scarfe was a sealer and had been part owner and captain of the *Agnes MacDonald*, a sealing schooner that was later wrecked off the coast of Japan. He became the captain for the Dunsmuir family, and in his eighties still lived at Tod Inlet aboard the *Mary S* – a handsome boat that had seen better days. In 1946 his foster daughter Mary (Lorna's mother) ordered him off his leaky vessel, fearing for the safety of the old sailor.

CHICKADEES CALL TO ONE ANOTHER above my head as they forage in the lichen and the licorice ferns decorating the leafless maple tree beside me. At first glance it seems that the moss, ferns and lichens are parasites, sapping the trees of their vitality as the introduced English ivy is prone to do, but this is not the case. These plants are epiphytic, explain Richard and Sydney Cannings in their book *British Columbia: A Natural History*. That is, they have formed a symbiotic relationship with the trees. The wet climate of our west coast leaches rainforests of nutrients, especially nitrates. Lichens, like the nubby lettuce lung lichen, convert atmospheric nitrogen into nitrates for the trees. Mosses and ferns perform the same function, but there are other partners, the mycorrhizae, which are less visible. The mycelia of certain soil fungi (including mushrooms) form the same relationship at root level. In exchange for the nutrition provided to its roots, the tree provides sugars from its leaves to the fungi. The lettuce lung lichens found around Tod Inlet are an indicator species for old-growth hemlock forests. The diversity of lichens increases after a forest is 150 to 200 years old and peaks at 350 years.

Lettuce lung lichen (*opposite and overleaf*).

A Beaver float plane drones as it gains elevation from Brentwood Bay. I hear voices and a young couple strolls by on the other side of the house foundation. This restful scene had a distinctly different feel during the early part of the twentieth century when the Vancouver Portland Cement Company was in full production. The area was stripped of its old-growth firs, and only a few scraggly trees dotted the land. The ground was often muddy, and the mining, breaking, burning and shipping of limestone was a constant reminder of the demands of industry. Black smoke spewed from the four chimney stacks. I imagine some of the everyday sounds: explosives fracturing limestone from the cliffs; steam engines powering bulldozers, tractors, shovels and ships; the scream of steel on steel as Chinese workers pushed the loaded carts along the rail line that linked the main quarry to the docks.

In 1980 Norm Parsell wrote a first-person account of the working conditions at the Wallace Drive quarry site, titled "A Nostalgic Excavation." Norm grew up at Tod Village, as his father came to work at the cement factory in 1907, only three years after it opened. Norm took a job there in March 1918, when he was 17. He wrote, "I was the fireman and craneman on a Marion steam shovel and my father was the engineer ... At that time we worked ten hours a day, six days a week. We were paid monthly, and for the first one I received $75. Then I went to $90 a month." In the article Norm expressed amazement "at the way the forest has grown up all around the area. At the time the quarry was operating the trees were mere saplings, but of course that was 61 years ago." He added that "a lot of the wood that we burned in the firebox for making steam was hauled there by Lorne Thomson's teams. More horses than trucks were used in that period."

He describes what a dangerous job it could be:

> There were two large and high wooden towers at each end of the quarry. A heavy, two-inch-diameter cable was deadheaded in the ground at the Benvenuto end and it stretched the length of the pit and over the tower at that end. There was a heavy cement deadhead here also and a turnbuckle with large bolts and nuts to tighten the cable.
>
> At this end of course was the bin into which the hoist operator dumped the skips of limestone, and below it the rock crusher. After the limestone was crushed it went onto a heavy conveyor belt which carried it across Wallace Drive. There it poured the rock into a very large bin. Large steel buckets were loaded which ran on sheaves on a heavy cable supported at intervals by strong wooden towers. The empty buckets came back on a lighter cable on the opposite side of these towers. This was the method to bring the limestone at least a mile to the old plant by Butchart Gardens.
>
> The hoist operator was high up in the control house and he could see down to the quarry floor. Two large cable drums powered by electric motors pulled the carriage with the rock skip back and forth, and lowered it to the quarry bottom.
>
> We would load the skip with limestone while the hoist man was dumping the other in the bin.

The last of four chimneys towers over the former factory site.
A close-up of the massive factory chimney, now 110 years old.

We had quite a smashup at the quarry while I was there. The four legs of each tower were 16 × 16 timbers with a lot of cross braces heavily bolted together where they crossed, and also bolted to the legs.

The loaded skip was high up over the quarry with eight tons of rock. All of a sudden the turnbuckle at the back of the tower fractured. The two-inch main cable end was fastened to a heavy steel piece in which there were two bolt holes to hold the turnbuckle.

When the steel became free it swung in toward the tower and when it caught the first cross timber, it hesitated a moment, then tore it away and carried on to the next one, and so on all the way up the tower.

The skip of rock came crashing down and the carriage went by my side of the steam shovel. It smashed into my boom engine and fractured a large gear. The big two-inch cable was strewn across the quarry floor. There was considerable damage and it took a month to get things fixed. Luckily no one was injured …

As one looks around here today, there is little indication that such an operation ever existed. But it does in the memory of anyone my age, and especially one who worked there so long ago.

There is a substantial ruin indicating that the operation Norm Parsell described did exist, but it is easy to miss. I discover it when I enter the park by an alternative trail only a few feet south of the main entrance on Wallace Drive. This entrance used to be a thin wedge into the forest, almost blocked by large boulders.

Above: A park entrance path just a few feet south of the main entrance. To the left of this trail are the many plinths that supported the overhead bucket line relay station that Norm Parsell described (p. 166).

Facing page: This gulley was blasted through in the days of the cement plant, probably to mine more clay and accommodate the railway to the clay mill, but Dem Carrier remembers a more bizarre history. This was the location for a scene from the 1935 Hollywood movie *Stampede*. Horses from the Sluggett and Thomson farms were stampeded through this narrow passage.

The old clay mill opposite the main falls of Tod Creek.

Now I see the ground worn through to the base of the boulders and a wide trail before me. I turn left to investigate, and the remarkable ruin is only steps off the trail. Mossy monoliths stand camouflaged in the verdant understorey of the woods. Initially I count eight pillars, eight feet tall and three feet square. As my eyes adjust, I see more, some square, some oblong – 15 in all. Steel hardware is still attached to the tops of the decaying concrete, and the long bolts with nuts attached sit like mechanical mushrooms in the moss below. These concrete blocks would have supported the main structure for the overhead buckets that carried the limestone to the plant after Norm Parsell and his co-workers had loaded them.

This haunting reminder of another time sits between the road and the dam and I decide to go down to the creek. There is no path and the ground is littered with old tin cans and industrial debris. At the creek's edge I stand on the narrow strip of fine black mud peppered with the tracks of Columbian black-tailed deer, and inhale the earthy odour of the still creek held above the dam. Choosing an easier route back up to the pillars, I discover a mound of light-coloured stones – a spill from one of the heavy buckets, dumped a century ago.

I walk the main pathway to the old clay mill and imagine the aerial line that would have traversed the forest on my right. The buckets of limestone were transported to the plant without power. Gravity forced the loaded carts downhill while bringing the empty carts back up to the loading station near Wallace Drive.

Stressed steel cable from the lines can still be found on the forest floor. There is an obvious ridge to the right of the main pathway, just before the old clay mill. This ridge also supported a narrow-gauge rail line that carried clay from the pit (north of the main entrance) near Wallace Drive to the old clay mill. All of the steel rails were salvaged about 60 years ago but I come across two small sections half-buried in the ground near a steep gully that was blasted out decades ago. The children of the area called this line the Toonerville Trolley, after a popular newspaper cartoon that ran from 1908–1955.

The old clay mill is a magnificent relic opposite the main falls of Tod Creek. I notice that a cut in the bank near the mill has a stream coursing through to Tod Creek. This diversion may have supplied water to turn the waterwheel that in turn provided the power to move the grindstone for the mill. In the 1930s and '40s a second deposit of clay was discovered up the hillside opposite the park entrance in what is now the Garden Estates subdivision. One of the homes accommodates a strange lawn ornament: a belted steel pulley seven feet in diameter that resembles a large flywheel. This location was a clay-washing station, providing clay for the manufacture of cement tiles and pots and for the Bamberton plant across the Inlet. From here a six-inch trough ran down the slope to where it was needed at the Inlet. The small manufacturing plant, called the "tile shed," was located on the land adjacent to the boatways.

In his article, Norm Parsell wrote that "sometime before the quarry was closed permanently a diamond drill outfit was brought in and drilled a lot of test holes to estimate the amount of limestone remaining. The tests were not too impressive, but they did drill into a lot of fresh water, which helps to keep the pond supplied for the (Brentwood Bay) water system today." Until 1981 an artesian spring in the limestone quarry on Wallace Drive was one of the water sources for Brentwood Bay. But Butchart Gardens, which owned the water rights to Tod Creek, had noticed that the less-than-pure water was becoming harmful to their plants and had an unpleasant odour. They negotiated with the municipality to allow the old quarry (sometimes called Quarry Lake) to be their new water supply. The growing Brentwood Bay area is now serviced by the Sooke reservoir.

I scramble back to the main pathway, seemingly alone. There is only one public entrance and I can usually gauge how many people are in the park by the number of cars by the roadside. I counted two on my way in and have passed two walkers and their dogs returning to their vehicles. A quiet thrill runs through me – am I the only one in the park? Not likely these days. My secret wish (and my fear) is to see a cougar, but this is unlikely too, as these stealthy prowlers are usually active only at night. Yet a friend of mine was walking down the trail on Mount Finlayson, which adjoins the park, when she realized she was being stalked by a cougar in broad daylight. Her dog was the target but that knowledge didn't prevent an adrenaline rush of fear. Luckily, she remembered her training and challenged the cougar rather than running down the trail as others might have

Each year more froth accumulates in the creek – no doubt a product of phosphates from nearby homes and industry.

done. Cougar sightings are not uncommon at Tod Inlet and the surrounding area, but no man or beast seems to be here on this quiet winter afternoon as I make my way to the bench that overlooks the Inlet. I watch as a belted kingfisher dives from one of the old concrete pilings. These same pilings supported the wharf for the steamships and railway in the early part of the twentieth century. Traditional wharf pilings, usually made from

These unused concrete pilings create a sculpture in the forest.

round, creosoted cedar timbers would never have lasted a hundred years. These are still vertical and little changed from the day they were embedded into the Inlet's floor. On land, adjacent to these pilings, about 50 of these reinforced Portland cement beams lie stockpiled and unused in the grass. With their pointed, rusty iron ends they resemble gigantic 50-foot pencils – Claes Oldenburg sculptures in the forest. Buffleheads appear and disappear, a cormorant slides into the water, a gull screams and the sound of a waterfall splashes behind me. This waterfall is actually the Butchart Gardens' Ross Fountain on the other side of the fence, in the original quarry that John Greig worked. Without coloured lights or fanfare it is going through the motions of its water-jet ballet in the silent winter Gardens.

After our recent rains, the waterfall from the dam is a wall of thundering ochre, mesmerizing in its intensity. Islands of foam the size of dining room tables collect in the back eddies, looking like gigantic lemon meringue pies complete with the darkened tips at the crests of the foam. I've been told that these accumulations of froth are a natural phenomenon, but I wonder. The powerful torrent of water in the centre of the stream flexes its muscles like a triumphant white serpent roaring its way to the sea. On a log suspended over the stream I spot an American dipper, its chunky body pumping up and down, oblivious to the deluge. I would be terrified to stand over this chaos, let alone hurl my four-inch body straight into it.

It's time to leave the park: it is getting late and the weather is deteriorating. The sky darkens as the sun drops behind the opposite hill, enveloped in cloud, and then the wind gusts forcefully, changes in pitch and becomes a frightening roar. Tall stands of firs around me sway their tops before the wind and then spring back in a swirling motion. I hope the heavy branches stay on the trees. The wind takes another run at the Inlet, and a distinctive sound vibrates through the trees again. My stomach tightens and I attempt to place this sound, this sensation. The gusting wind makes it dangerous to be here, but I'm rooted, taking in the charged atmosphere. Something holds my attention – an otherworldly sound that is both high-pitched and roaring at the same time. Then I remember. On a trek in Nepal many years ago, a small group of us were holed up in a stone hut on Everest's southeast side waiting out a two-day snowstorm. On the third day we emerged to a blue and white world. It was then that I heard the eerie sound – the atmospheric jet stream howling across the roof of the world ten thousand feet above us. Few of us today, myself included, experience the gut-wrenching fear of Mother Nature in full force as we live our cosseted lives, the kind of fear that turns to awe, then respect and finally acknowledgement of our humble position in the hierarchy of life on earth.

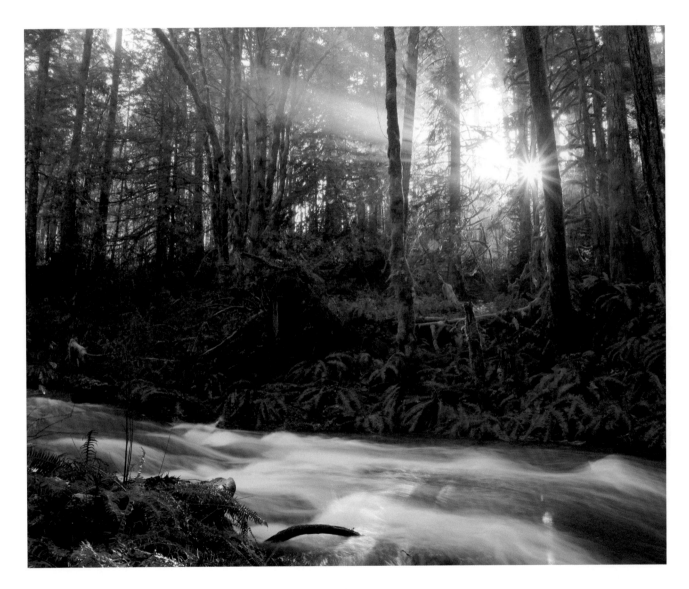

Winter   177

This humility has guided the actions of the Salish people for millennia. Every aspect of life was circumscribed by gratitude to the natural world and belief that the fish, birds and animals needed for sustenance were also beloved ancestors. One of their most poignant observances is the Children's Salmon Ceremony described in the book *Reef Net Technology of the Saltwater People*, by Earl Claxton Sr. and John Elliott Sr. Upon the arrival of the first catch of salmon from the reef nets, the elders built a firepit onshore. Near the pit, a bed was prepared to receive the salmon: ferns, duck down, red earth, consumption plants and cherry bark were layered in the bed. Young children cradled the salmon like babies, with the head of the fish resting on their left arm. As they made their way from the canoe to the bed and firepit, they limped to indicate how weak they would be without the nourishment of the salmon. The elders sang a special song to greet their relatives, the first salmon of the year. After the salmon feast, the bones were gathered in a basket and the children returned them to the sea with respect and thanks.

WALKERS ARE EVERYWHERE on this first Sunday after New Year's Day, basking in the lambent sunshine. My boots sound a hollow tap on the frozen ground and I inhale the sharp fresh air as I make my way down to the stream through ferns, salal and maple leaves, all embroidered with frost. In a shady bend of the wintry freshet, several downed conifers, festooned with rows of icicles, jut out into the stream. I arrive at the clearing overlooking the Inlet and my eyes tear up as I try to focus on the brilliance that is Tod Inlet today. Yesterday only a thin sheet of ice glazed the water, but today it is littered with the rocks that children have tossed in an effort to break its tough surface. Gulls skate unsteadily and three sailboats sit locked in its grip. From today's perspective, spring seems barely possible, yet here it is, like a held breath, and without prejudice it waits.

In the last days of winter the evergreen branches are tipped with new growth, the underbrush is budding and bulbs are shooting spears through the moss. Even though windstorms may blow through, hail may pelt the forest or a late frost may shroud the Inlet, nothing will halt the insistence of spring. Columbian black-tailed deer will grow new antlers, lizards will sun themselves in the shell middens and mallard drakes will chase their mates.

The salmon may not be setting out to sea after wintering in the eelgrass meadows, the blue grouse may not be perching heavily in the trees and the elk may not be roaming the hills with their new calves, but Nature's grace is still compelling. She heals us all.

On a foggy day, people and animals appear to be posing for a diorama by Vancouver artist Jeff Wall.

Acheson, Laurie Williamson, and Morley Eldridge. "Archaeological Resource Overview of the Gowlland Range/Tod Inlet Commonwealth Nature Legacy Protected Area." Report prepared for BC Parks, Ministry of Environment, Lands and Parks, March 31, 1995.

Alexander, Maureen, and Andrew S. Brown. *Bamberton: From Dust to Bust and Back*. Mill Bay, BC: Bamberton Historical Society, 2012.

Allen, Anne. *Prospect Lake Reflections: A Photographic Tribute of Significant Heritage Stories*. Victoria, BC: Prospect Lake Heritage Society, 2012.

"Art 'Interfaces' Life." *Sidney Review*, June 30, 2004. (References "100 Bloomin' Years for Butchart Gardens," by Judy Reimche.)

BC Parks 2010/2011 Annual Report." Victoria: BC Ministry of Environment, 2011. Accessed 2015-02-15 (pdf) at http://is.gd/4Fnhmy.

Berger, Carol. "Boaters Mourn Loss of Lovely Tod Inlet." *Sidney Review*, January 14, 1981.

Cannings, Richard, and Sydney Cannings. *British Columbia: A Natural History*. 2nd ed. revised and updated. Vancouver: Greystone Books, 2004.

——. *The B.C. Roadside Naturalist*. Vancouver: Greystone Books, 2002.

Clarke, David. *The Butchart Gardens: A Family Legacy*. Victoria, BC: Butchart Gardens Ltd., 2003.

Claxton, Earl Sr., and John Elliott Sr. *Reef Net Technology of the Saltwater People*. Brentwood Bay, BC: Saanich Indian School Board, 1994.

"Deo Volente I" (blogpost). *Life in the Philippines*, March 2, 2010. Accessed 2015-02-20 at http://malate-silang.blogspot.ca/2010/03/deo-volente.html.

First Nations: Land Rights and Environmentalism in British Columbia. Website researched, written, compiled, formatted, hyperlinked and encoded by Dr. Karen Wonders, Research Fellow, Institute for the History of Science, University of Goettingen, Germany, 2008. Accessed 2015-02-20 at www.firstnations.eu.

"Funeral Pyre Ready for Tar Gool Singh." *Victoria Daily Colonist*, April 12, 1907, 10. Accessed 2015-02-20 at http://is.gd/PYoiyw.

Gowlland Tod Provincial Park Trail Map." Victoria: BC Parks, "08/01." Accessed 2015-02-15 (pdf) at http://is.gd/dz3Eq3.

Gray, David R. "Deep and Sheltered Waters: A Preliminary Report on the History and Ecology of Tod Inlet, British Columbia." Report prepared by Grayhound Information Services, October 2001.

——. "Pigs' Teeth, Pottery and Portland Cement: The Story of the Chinese Workers of Tod Inlet, BC." *This Country Canada* 9 (Autumn 1995/Winter 1996): 56–67.

——. "Searching for the Sikhs of Tod Inlet." Posted to the Film/Stage section of Sikhchic.com in 2007. Accessed 2015-02-20 at http://is.gd/auXQCq.

Harrington, Jane. *An Archaeological and Historical Overview of Limeburning in Victoria*. Melbourne, Australia: Heritage Council Victoria, 2000.

Hebda, Richard. "Ecological Values of Tod Inlet Development Proposal Lands." Pamphlet. Royal BC Museum, May 1991.

"Industrial Lime Burning." *Out of Oblivion: A Landscape through Time* (website). Yoredale, Bainbridge, Leyburn, North Yorkshire, UK: Yorkshire Dales National Park Authority, 2015. Accessed 2015-02-20 at www.outofoblivion.org.uk/ind_lime.asp.

Ingram, Ben. "Monarch Butterflies Becoming Rare in BC," *Nanaimo Daily News*, March 15, 2013. Accessed 2015-02-20 at http://is.gd/vTqE7h.

Islands of British Columbia Conference 2004: An Interdisciplinary Exploration. Graham Brazier, Nick Doe and Lorraine Martinuik, eds. Denman Island, BC: Arts Denman 2005.

Keddie, Grant. "The Archaeological Remains of Tod Inlet." Pamphlet. Royal BC Museum, 1991.

Ladner, Peter. "The Stream Saviours." *Monday Magazine*, December 19–25, 1985.

Lavoie, Judith. "Today's Lake Tomorrow's Dump? Highlands Landfill Might Even Be Future Golf Course, Engineers Say." Victoria *Times Colonist*, January 25, 1986.

Lillard, Charles. "A Scots Boy Retires to Victoria." Victoria *Times Colonist*, May 1, 1993.

———. *Seven Shillings a Year: The History of Vancouver Island.* Ganges, BC: Horsdal & Schubart, 1986.

Lincoff, Gary H. *National Audubon Society Field Guide to North American Mushrooms.* New York: Alfred A. Knopf, 1981.

Lloyd, Kitty. "Restoration Project: Tod Inlet, 2004." Unpublished ms.

Mallard, Derrick. "In Memoriam Gwen Mallard." *Vancouver Sun*, December 8, 1999. Reprint accessed 2015-02-20 at www.vcn.bc.ca/spec/spec/Spectrum/winter1999/page20.html.

"Management Plan for Gowlland Tod Provincial Park." BC Parks, Ministry of Environment, Lands and Parks, 1996. Accessed 2015-02-15 (pdf) at http://is.gd/mP5xeQ.

Manchur, Jan. "A Historical Look at Tod Inlet, 1904–1921." *Peninsula Times*, November 2008, 24.

McConnaughey, Bayard H., and Evelyn McConnaughey. *Pacific Coast.* Audubon Society Nature Guides. New York: Alfred A. Knopf, 1984.

Miller, William. "Tod Inlet Property Bought for $7.2-million." Victoria *Times Colonist*, March 14, 1989.

Morrison, Brad. "Captain Thomas Pritchard, Pioneer and Adventurer." *Peninsula News Review*, February 10, 1999, 18–19.

———. "John Greig: He Fiddled While the Limestone Burned." *Beachcomber*, January 28, 1998, 7.

Nathan, Holly. "Saanich Inlet Right for Marine Park." Victoria *Times Colonist*, January 31, 1990.

———. "What's Pristine about Tod Inlet, Developer Asks." Victoria *Times Colonist*, October 4, 1990, G1.

Parsell, Mary. "Reminiscences of Tod Inlet." *Peninsula News Review*, 1958.

Parsell, T.N. "A Nostalgic Excavation." *The Islander*, 1980.

Pojar, Jim, and Andy MacKinnon, *Plants of Coastal British Columbia.* Rev. ed. Vancouver: Lone Pine publishing, 2004.

Potter, Sheila. "Where Has All the Eel Grass Gone? *Marina Mirror*, August 20, 2000, 13–14.

Preston, Dave. *The Story of Butchart Gardens*. Victoria, BC: Highline Publishing, 1996.

"Robert Pim Butchart (1856–1943)" Masonic biography. Grand Lodge of British Columbia and Yukon A.F. & A.M. Accessed 2015-02-20 at http://is.gd/q1Xt8R.

"Saanich Inlet" (archived webpage). Fisheries and Oceans Canada, 2009. Accessed 2015-02-20 at http://is.gd/GJGgPD.

"Saanich Inlet" (webpage). Ocean Networks Canada, Victoria, BC, 2014. Accessed 2015-02-20 at http://is.gd/vFb2Cw.

Sept, J. Duane. *Common Mushrooms of the Northwest: Alaska, Western Canada & Northwestern United States*. Rev. ed. Sechelt, BC: Calypso Publishing, 2012.

Sluggett, Larry. *Brentwood Pioneer: The Life and Times of John Sluggett, 1829–1909*. Brentwood Bay, BC: Self-published, 2000.

Smith, William. "Old Native Agreement May Stall Tod Proposal." Victoria *Times Colonist*, March 31, 1982.

Swinburne, Margaret. "The Man from Tod Inlet." *The Review*, May 4, 1988, 14.

Tamburri, Valerie. "Historic Tod Inlet Has Healed Itself from Industrial Past." *The Review*, July 29, 1992, 4–5.

Thompson, Sarah. "Tod Creek Chinese Led Difficult Lives." *The Review*, 1987.

"Tod Creek Flats Integrated Management Plan." Report prepared by Murdoch de Greef Inc. for the District of Saanich and the Friends of Tod Creek Watershed, November 2009. Accessed 2015-02-15 (pdf) at http://is.gd/RNmj7X.

"Tradition in Felicities." Royal BC Museum exhibit celebrating 155 years of Victoria's Chinatown, February 7 to September 29, 2013.

Turner, Nancy J. *Food Plants of Coastal First Peoples*. Victoria and Vancouver: Royal BC Museum and UBC Press, 1995.

Turner, Nancy J., and Richard J. Hebda. *Saanich Ethnobotany: Culturally Important Plants of the W̱SÁNEĆ People*. Victoria: Royal BC Museum, 2012.

Union of BC Indian Chiefs. "Historical Timeline from the 1700s to Present." Webpage. Vancouver and Kamloops, 2010. Accessed 2015-02-20 at www.ubcic.bc.ca/Resources/timeline.htm.

Walbran, John T. *British Columbia Coast Names 1592–1906: To Which Are Added a Few Names in Adjacent United States Territory: Their Origin and History*. Vancouver: Douglas & McIntyre, 1971. First published by the Geographic Board of Canada, 1909. Heritage page scans available at www.ourroots.ca/e/page.aspx?id=736704.

Ward-Harris, Joan. *More Than Meets the Eye: The Life and Lore of Western Wildflowers*. Toronto: Oxford University Press, 1983.

Werkman, Glen. "Tod Inlet Could Become Bluegrouse Regional Park." *The Review*, June 12, 1991.

Wright, Nikki. "Focus on Tod Inlet at February 15 Meeting." *Peninsula News Review*, February 14, 2007, A16.

Wright, Nikki, and Ana Simeon. "Undersea Meadows: Eelgrass Provides a Nursery for Sea Life." *Monday Magazine*, June 3–9, 2010.

ACKNOWLEDGMENTS

I want to thank everyone who generously donated their time, their memories and their knowledge with me. Many thanks to Vera Ferguson, Kathleen Lane, Lorna Kenyon, Mary Gilbert, Dr. Grant Keddie, Earl Claxton Jr., David Clarke, John Elliott Sr., Lorna Pugh, Garry McKevitt, Kitty Lloyd, Dr. Bob Griffin, Dr. Marji Johns, Ron and Diana dePol, Reg Barber, Dr. Richard Hebda, Steve Acheson, Mary Haig-Brown, Ian Bruce, Don Sluggett, Bradley Williams, Susan Langlois, Dan Carrier, Desmond (Dem) Carrier, John Creviston, Tony Heeley, Lise Gentile, Winona (Noni) Pugh, Donyne Grey, Lis Bailly and Arlene Curry. A special thank you to John Grey for flying me over Tod Inlet in his Cessna to take the aerial shots.

I am very grateful for the support of Nikki Wright and Sarah Verstegen of SeaChange Marine Conservation Society. Thank you for making your archives available to me and for being such enthusiastic supporters of my project.

Thank you Audrey McClellan for your sensitive and intelligent editing. It was a joy to work with you.

Last but not least, I want to thank Don Gorman, publisher at RMB | Rocky Mountain Books for taking on this first time author, Frances Hunter for designing such an exquisite book and Chyla Cardinal for the cover design.